Father,
Child,
Water

Father,
Child,
Water

poems

GARY DOP

Red Hen Press | *Pasadena, CA*

Book layout by Danielle Verde

Library of Congress Cataloging-in-Publication Data

Dop, Gary.

[Poems. Selections]

Father, child, water : poems / Gary Dop.—First edition.

    pages cm

ISBN 978-1-59709-422-1 (pbk.)

I. Title.

PS3604.O68A6 2015

811'.6—dc23

                    2014037124

The National Endowment for the Arts, the Los Angeles County Arts Commission, the Dwight Stuart Youth Fund, the Los Angeles Department of Cultural Affairs, the Pasadena Arts & Culture Commission and the City of Pasadena Cultural Affairs Division, Sony Pictures Entertainment, and the Ahmanson Foundation partially support Red Hen Press.

First Edition

Published by Red Hen Press

www.redhen.org

Acknowledgments

Many of the poems in this collection appeared in the following publications:

2River View, "That Night in Mobridge"; *Agni*, "Evander Holyfield's Left Ear Remembers June 28, 1997," "At 78, Maurita Discovers the Waterslide"; *Anti-Poetry*, "Coleman Generator Plant—Darrell, Line Supervisor"; *Blue Earth Review*, "Guys Like Me," "Minneapolis Snow," "To the Ice Cream Man"; *Burntdistrict*, "Destroying a Church Potluck"; *Cave Wall*, "Bill Bitner's Bundle of Something Identical," "Bill Bitner Smells"; *Center*, "Bill Bitner Delivers Pizza"; *Coachella Review*, "You Can Call Me Al"; *Green Mountains Review*, "Poverty Identification Simulation"; *New Letters*, "Father, Child, Water"; *New York Quarterly*, "The Long Madness"; *Ninth Letter*, "Bill Bitner Day Dreams"; *Other Poetry (UK)*, "Shifting the Bolt"; *Passages North*, "Bill Bitner Attends his Grandfather's Funeral"; *Pilgrimage*, "Northern Peru"; *Platte Valley Review*, "The Spotted Owl"; *Poetry City USA Anthology*, "A Brief Argument," "Elegy for Thomas Kinkade, Painter of Lite"; *Poetry East*, "The Spit Hand"; *Poetry Northwest*, "Xerxes' Queen"; *Prairie Schooner*, "The Girl with No Nightmares"; *Quiddity*, "Pothead Pete's English Presentation"; *Rattle*, "Poem of 4 Explanations of Poems at Poetry Readings"; *Salamander*, "To My Love Handles"; *Salt Hill*, "After the Tornado of '62, Indianola, Iowa"; *South Dakota Review*, "Winter Campout," "Little Girl, Little Lion"; *Sow's Ear Poetry Review*, "My Uncle Learns Me How to Keep a Mechanic . . ."; *Sugar House Review*, "Bill Bitner Meets Subway's Jared," "Have You Seen the Santa Lion?" "Theologians"; *Sycamore Review*, "Amish Man in the Andy Warhol Museum," "How to Pretend You've Read Moby Dick"; *Tiger's Eye: A Journal of Poetry*, "The Northern Mississippi"; *What Light Poetry Contest (mnLIT)*, "Bill Bitner at the Henry Doorly Zoo"; and *Whistling Shade*, "On Swearing."

"To the Ice Cream Man" received a Special Mention in the 2011 Pushcart Prize Anthology. *American Life in Poetry*, the Poetry Foundation's syndicated newspaper column, reprinted "On Swearing" and "Father, Child, Water" in recent columns.

Thank you to my wife Liz—good kisser, gracious reader, great mom, and adventure guide—the best person I've known. I am yours.

Thanks to my fierce and lovely daughters: Brooklyn, Amorie, and Juliette.

Thanks to my new family at Randolph College—*vita abundantior*.

Thanks to my gracious Minneapolis friends at North Central University. To my comrades at the University of Nebraska MFA program, especially my mentors: Ted Kooser, Teri Youmans Grimm, Richard Robbins, and William Trowbridge.

Thanks to the friends who have picked at these poems: Carrie Helmberger, Jerry VanIeperen, Chris Fletcher, Brian White, Jason Freeman, Michael Scott Rash, Desiree Libengood, and Leslie Crabtree. And to editor Erika Stevens, *Buch Zauberer*.

Thanks to the great beast of Southern California, the Red Hen Press—Kate, Mark, Sam, William, Alisa, Kim, and Gabi—for taking a chance on this new ripple.

To the wonderful organizations that have recognized and invested in my work and life: *Rain Taxi*, the University of Minnesota, the NE Summer Honors Program, the University of Nebraska at Kearney, *The Pushcart Prize Anthology*, *American Life in Poetry*, Banfil-Locke Center for the Arts, the Great Plains Writer's Conference, the University of South Dakota, and Sigma Tau Delta English Honor Society.

Thanks to my wife's people, who have loved me anyway. To my parents and sisters, who inflicted just enough suffering to push me toward poetry. To my mother, who, when I was in grade school, taught me and my friends using writing workshops— so much is your fault.

And Dylan Thomas said it best: "These poems, with all their crudities, doubts, and confusions, are written for the love of man and in praise of God, and I'd be a damn' fool if they weren't."

for Liz

Contents

III.

WATERSHED

Shadows That Might Catch Fire

I.
Father

FATHER, CHILD, WATER

I lift your body to the boat
before you drown or choke or slip too far

beneath. I didn't think—just jumped, just did
what I did like the physics

that flung you in. My hands clutch under
year-old arms, between your life

jacket and your bobbing frame, pushing you,
like a fountain cherub, up and out.

I'm fooled by the warmth pulsing from
the gash on my thigh, sliced wide and clean

by an errant screw on the stern.
No pain. My legs kick out blood below.

My arms strain
against our deaths to hold you up

as I lift you, crying, reaching, to the boat.

Bin Laden's Rug

My wife says, *It's a rug. It's my rug.*
Honey, that's our rug. Strange
to watch the room of the dead man,
his rug, blotched in blood, the same rug
that lies lifeless by my own
disheveled bed. This is the rug I bled on,
stumbling in my sleep, splitting open
my toe. With the new day's rumblings
of SEALs and clips of what the news calls
blood on the carpet, we walk, hand in hand,
like nobody does in the safety of home,
to our bedroom to see Bin Laden's rug.
My daughter, born into the white noise
of terror, scurries past us to pounce
from the old imported rug to the unmade bed.
I hold her back, not knowing why.
The TV's off. We watch our viral rug.
Tonight I'll kneel to look for something
under the bed, my face touching
the rough maroon threads, perhaps
from the same loom as his. The world
will unravel, and I'll wonder what my hands
search for in the darkness.

SHIFTING THE BOLT

The sun hasn't risen, the deer haven't fallen,
and Dad hasn't stopped reliving the dead
whitetail of his youth as we drive the two hours

to Red Willow county. We eat at a hunter's café,
easy eggs and bacon thick as steak. In an open field
near the frozen river, he points to my spot

and walks silently through a draw and over
the shadow of a bank. The sun yawns. We hear two
distant shots, then a late third. In the dim dawn,

we walk back to the truck to drive to another
open space. I unload my Mauser, the gun my father
first used. Shifting the bolt toward me, I ask

if he hunted with his father. He lifts his gun
to his shoulder and tests the sight on the horizon.

How to Pretend You've Read *Moby-Dick*

Nothing exists in itself.
> —Melville, *Moby-Dick*

Pause, as though considering the sea.
Consider the sea. Cup your hands
in a shell over your ear. Say, "I'm considering

the sea." Your inquisitors will feel slight,
like a ship pestering the seas, hunting you,
your wisdom a great whale. As they grapple

with your unexpected waves, reconsider
the sea. Say, "I can't even think of the name
of the ship or the captain." They'll smell blood

and squeal *Pequod* and *Ahab,* assuming
they've harpooned you. Just then,
channeling the inconstant sea, spring forward

and say, "I spoke metaphorically
in the persona of the sea, which casts aside,
swallows, and dismisses the existence

of Ahab and that ship." If you've lured them,
add, "I might also suggest that the sea,
mother of our prehistoric fathers, drowns

and defies these shallow discussions."
Finally, gaze two inches to the right
of their eye, as though you've lost

something precious in their ear.

When they respond, ignore them, and whisper,

"We're all Ishmael. *Call me Ishmael.*"

Minneapolis Snow

Like cold beer
poured

from the clouds,
she falls,

foams,
softens

the cold,

the city's
edge.

SPOTTED OWL

The War on Terror, 2001–

In the first few hours of the century, we hunted
like spotted owls, swooping and striking
desert mice scattered in the sands of night.

As the sun rises in the time to come, we'll look
down at our own corpse: tiny bones
and loose flesh still fixed to distant joints

where our beak couldn't reach as we pecked
away our feathers and fed on our fat under
the dusty stars, so sure we clutched an enemy.

LITTLE GIRL, LITTLE LION

From the stool above our soaking dishes, she proclaims,
I can never be a poet, like it's written on a sacred stone

in her identity's medieval cathedral. I am her father.
She does not turn to me. *Why?* I ask, pulling wrinkled hands

out of the suds we share. The blue glass she's holding slips
under the water to a hollow clank. Touching her wet elbows,

I hear, *Daddy, girls can't be poets.* I've never thought
about how my daughter mirrors herself in Mommy

who doesn't write. I say the right things, pull her away
from the sink to the floor, and bend to look in her

searching eyes, brown like her mother's. They ask, *Are you
sure?* I rush away to find Bishop, Rich, Sexton, Dickinson—

any girl on the shelves above *Where the Wild Things Are.*
Showing her the stack, she pulls out Plath and opens to

"Daddy." I snatch the book back like it's rat poison.
Again, I can't be trusted. Can I be trusted? How can I

wrecking-ball the commandments she's constructed? I read
the opening stanza which ends in a sneeze,

and she's satisfied. *More Sylvia later,* I say. *Oh Darling,*
you'll be whatever you need to be, and if it's Poet,

the world will learn to welcome your wild words, cathedrals
will crumble, stars supernova, and nothing

that pretends will remain—but your words are water,
your life a metaphor only you complete. I say all this,

our backs resting against the cold oven.

THE ONLY MAN IN IOWA WITH FIVE CANNONS

I dream of my father in an open green field
surrounded by his five cannons, four facing the four winds
and one facing him, his hand clenching each lanyard.

His eye twitches, scans the horizon for enemy.
My father, the retired soldier, collects wars:
Cannons, Bombs, Bullets he never fired in battle.

Maybe my father's the only Marine who wanted
Vietnam but got stuck stateside training grunts,
guarding guns, testing his aim on nothing smarter

than a deer, nothing that knows death
as more than a scent, nothing that shoots back, nothing
to test the worth of a soldier who will learn

to collect cannons in Iowa and wonder if he would've
run, if he would've killed, if he would've been given
a warrior's name. His brothers envy his innocence,

which fires its own burning shells. I dream of cannons
melting into the dew and him walking free
in the field of open dreams. I dream

my father pulls four worn cords, and we
wake to our world without want of cannons.

"You Can Call Me Al"

The song's video should have a poem
so you'll watch the pink room
again. Maybe you'll YouTube it. I don't
care, just get the rhythm
of the silliness
before 3-ounce liquids in airline bags
and turban fear. Remember
how we used to sing a silly song
we didn't understand before we sang
the soldier song we knew wasn't true? I think
Chevy Chase should write the poem—
I'm Chevy Chase and you're not
America anymore—so we have a figure,
Chevy Chase, we can trust, a *soft-in-the-middle*
role model singing purity
in uncertainty, someone to pick up
the trumpet.

To My Love Handles

The body's seers, you prophesy
to the left, to the right, where the rest of me—
my loves—will go. Lead me,

guide me, walk beside me. I sneak cookies
in the night to strip off the guilt
of the South Beach sin that enslaves me
and threatens your lives. Together,

we flow into the wide world,
our promised land of whole milk and honey
butter. We pass on Norwegian girth

to my children and my children's children.
Surgery, they say, can suck you
into a lab jar, but who would
hold me when the nights are cold,

feed me when the meals
are thin, lead me into my future?
Forgive the fat tire blasphemy—nothing

spare in love. When you were given
your God-given name, I stood, silhouetted
on a mountainside, my hands beside me,
holding you, you holding me. This bony,

emaciated world, fat on lean lies, persecutes
the free, and envies, in secret, our corpulent
days without counting calories. Someday

when I'm dead on the catafalque,
my children surrounding, comforted
by your growing kin, I'll lie there
upheld by my dearest, my nearest friends.

Guys Like Me

I'm the kind of guy who cried at *Top Gun*
when Tom Cruise held Goose's helmeted head,
hanging loose, dead, cracked by the hatch.
Don't get me wrong, I cheered

when Tom blew up the Russians,
but I tear up when Goose comes back to life
as a bald doctor on *ER*. He's doing CPR
and I picture Tom on the aircraft carrier tossing

dog tags in the wimpling ocean. The world
isn't made for men
who don't want to watch the end
of *Steel Magnolias* for fear that Julia Roberts

is gonna die, again. When I open a beer
with my buddies while we fix messy stuff
on our cars, I pretend to care
about the Bears—Will they ever have

a decent Quarterback, and will that Tight End
get over his groin pull? They don't let me ask
if *Beaches* is based on a true story
so I can know if I need to weep. I get greased up

with the best of them, but I keep a clean sleeve
for whenever Meg Ryan looks up
for Goose, whenever Sally Field
can't save Shelby, and whenever

Bette Midler—who I usually hate—sings "Wind
Beneath My Wings." In Heaven
there'll be a sports bar where the big screen's
only channel is Lifetime.

DESTROYING A CHURCH POTLUCK

Besides bringing steak only for yourself, find both ladies
who brought potato salad, and ask, *Which of you forgot
to cook the potatoes?* Smile, so your perceived naïveté
will stoke the foul flames, which spread in whispers

across the linoleum fellowship hall: *Sweetheart,
are my potatoes hard? Clarisse uses too much mustard,
don't you think?* Soon the creamed corn soufflé ladies
will measure their leftovers and encourage, with elbows,

their husbands to return to the plastic, eight-foot tables.
The men will dip from each other's wife's soufflé—
an act of potluck adultery. You should point this out
while asking each corn lady, *Does your husband work late?*

Spill something red near the gal who glides back
and forth, kitchen to table, like she's carrying blood
to battle. When she bends to clean up say, *Gee thanks,
too bad there's a lack of variety this year.* Suggest

that in honor of Luther they replace the lemonade
with a bold beer. Ask the pastor's wife, after she's sat
to eat from the pickings, *Are you gonna get more gals
involved so we can do this right like the last pastor's wife?*—

she worked so hard. Smile, and before she responds,
ask about vegan options, burp, and tear into your T-bone.

Theologians

They heard a man made a boat with holes
on the waterline, seven in the bow, three
in the port, and one in the stern. When
she sailed, she took on water but never
sank. They came for the ride, laughed,
and looked for the trick of how she soaked
in the waves but sailed true. For a season,
they didn't complain about her shoddy sail
or the holes. Then, as men do, they voted,
in grand landside committees, to patch
the open spaces with good wood,
insisting on the sanctity of a dry deck
and hull. The boat sank,
so they built a better boat, no holes,
to lift the dead from the depths, to drag her
to shore to anchor their stories of sailing
with holes. She's sideways now, half-buried
in sand and weeds. A few of them remember
their wet feet with a sea-sick nostalgia
that brings them, late in the star-plagued night,
to remove their shoes as they sift themselves
through the sand and approach the starboard
of their grounded, still-sunken ship.
The good ones come here to die.

ELEGY FOR THOMAS KINKADE,
PAINTER OF LITE

Last week in an upscale hotel
restroom, I saw the light

from the round windows of cottages
touched up with snow. I stood

at the urinal, holding
your pastoral image, yellow

splashing from the sunny clouds
on the sunny river

and the sunny town.
My head tilted

to the side, I leaned forward
and felt the light

on my black shoes.

THE SPIT HAND

He spat on the ground and made mud with the saliva
and spread the mud on the man's eyes.
 —The Gospel of John

Mud on my eyes, I saw men as trees
walking their sway behind a veil
of rain, and this in-between was enough,

when I'd seen more in a moment
than in 37 years—sweet blur
as his spit hand touched me

a second time, and crisp trees
held their ground as men walked
away, stiff, afraid of the clarity

I never asked for but needed
to live like a blind man who sees.

ON SWEARING

In Normandy, at Pointe Du Hoc,
where some Rangers died,
Dad pointed to an old man
20 feet closer to the edge than us,
asking if I could see
the medal the man held
like a rosary.
As we approached the cliff
the man's swearing, each bulleted
syllable, sifted back
toward us in the ocean wind.
I turned away,
but my shoulder was held still
by my father's hand,
and I looked up at him
as he looked at the man.

II.
Child

To the Ice Cream Man

I got no green money for your red,
white, and blue bomb pops. You say
they're delectable, and delectable,
I think, means a thousand dime-cicles
plus sugar sparkles. I tasted it
in my head. You said *only*
really hard, *only one dollar*,
like dollars is dimes and everybody
can get delectables any time, but
Mom says since Dad got his slip
from Ford we won't have steaks
on Sundays or probably
new backpacks or those shoes
that light up on the back part
when you run. Dad likes
fudge pops and beer. I can run
like lightening, faster than your truck
and your bell. If I grow up
I'll drive a fast car with an ice cream
freezer in the back seat. Nobody
likes your bell.

After the Tornado of '62, Indianola, Iowa

Barbara, the 4H cow, lumbers in a circle
around the empty trough. The boy finds
his no-jump pony Trigger grazing

two fences and fields away. The clouds pull
the moldy sky toward Pickard's Park
as the boy and his father walk in silence

through the mess of farm, the milk barn split
to splinters and stones. Beside the pig barn,
the boy's hand glides along

the top edge of fence till he stops
stiff, a foot away from a pigeon
with no tail feathers. The bird

quivers. Its plucky legs cling
to the whitewashed wood.
Later, when the stars crack open

the night, the boy crawls
from his second-story window
hauling worms from his bait box

to the spot on the fence
where nothing remains. It's too dark
to see anything dead on the ground.

HAVE YOU SEEN THE SANTA LION

that leaves a shadow on Brad's lawn? It's stood
since his brother Bo died in the river
on the loop home from Viki's Bar
and Bait seven years ago. Brad sold

his Thunderbird with t-tops to pay
eight thousand bucks to a bronze artist
in Toledo. A nine-foot slab
poured on his trailer's front lawn

anchors the beast to earth. After the neighbors
crowbarred-up the back legs, Brad looped
an old boat chain over its back
and welded it to the trailer. For Christmas

he sticks a red hat on the head. The lion's wild
mane catches the snow, and people drive down
the dead end to see the Santa Lion
in the trailer court. Brad sits on his stoop

with an empty shotgun and a twelve pack
waiting for a fight. When the snow falls off
the lion's beard and the cars don't come,
the roaring begins and lasts deep into the night.

The Girl with No Nightmares

*Creativity now is as important in education
as literacy, and we should treat it with the same status.*
    —Sir Ken Robinson

So the girl they've been protecting, the one
they've kept at the clean brick house on the hill
surrounded by the scenic pine trees to the west,
the pristine green fields with no power

lines to the south and east, and Crystal Lake
to the north, she's changed. They didn't
tell her about the war, the sick kids
in the village, or the price of the air

purifier, her tutors, and the irradiated food.
Everyone wears gloves. They keep conflict
away. It's expensive to make the food
healthy and taste like she likes, to bend

light so it's a hot day when she wants the sun,
to find a plot for a new, fun story without fear
and dragons. She believed everything
about their world and never heard the shears

at night clipping the silent lawn or her split ends.
But last week, she woke shaking and screaming,
screaming about angels. She doesn't know
demons or devils or the way paint chips

from walls. To her white room, they rushed
calmly with the hushed clowns
and the happy juice, but she screamed, bit
the makeup face, and invented words. She screamed

until the doctor pilled her and listened to how
the angels quit singing. *The angels quit singing?*
he asked. *Not yet, but they will*, she trembled,
tapping her curly-haired head against the wainscoting.

Darling, there's no conflict in the world—the angels
will always sing. He inflicted a smile. *No, no*, she said,
Ten thousand years from now on a Tuesday, they'll quit
singing for a while, less than a second, a blink, half

a blink, no singing. There will be no singing,
and I think I'll go far away from this dream
you've locked me inside. With that, she cried,
and clinging to her sides, she fell asleep and hasn't woken.

No, no, I'm joking, I lied. She's eating well, playing
well, thinking their happy thoughts, and she has no idea
the angels will quit singing.

Amish Man in the Andy Warhol Museum

I am a deeply superficial person.
   —Andy Warhol

Don't stand with your back to the art,
the perky volunteer, glasses down
on her nose, said to the students horseshoed

around her. She stood, her back
to the *Campbell's Soup*, claiming she knew
how to respect the art. *A kid in New York City*

put his gum on a painting, so we don't allow—
I couldn't hear anymore when the Amish man
bent down at the pink squares

in *Electric Chair*. I wanted to see his face,
but I settled for the reflection of a bearded smile
on a *Silver Cloud* Mylar balloon. I wanted

to hear what he whispered at *White Burning Car*
to remember my artsy high school teacher, a former
Mennonite, flipping yellowed slides, bemoaning

the state of art. The Amish man ignored most of
the silver but stopped long enough to find the falling man
in *Suicide (silver jumping man)*. Truth be told,

I saw nothing of the Amish man—he'd left
as I first entered the oversized front doors. Maybe he'd wept
at the *Portraits of Jews*. Maybe the *Brillo Pads* or the *Jesus*

Punching Bags gave him pause. Maybe he'd never
been beyond the front booth once he heard the price.
But I wanted a poem. My lying, line by line, began

as he disappeared down the uncobbled street, my back
to Warhol's head: great, terrible, and looking down.

A Brief Argument

The hunter, my father, a Marine, pops two shots
at a young buck from too far. His hands motion
for me to march the pasture and stand
on the ridge. At the edge, overlooking

the brown brush, I spot the deer
thirty feet, no more, down the embankment.
He stares at me, as if to say, *I know why
we're here*, but when I pull my first shot,

which smokes up the dirt, he doesn't run.
I want to run. We're both too young
for decisions that might save us.
He takes two steps, his black hole eyes

on me, my breath held, my fingers shaking,
my cheek tight against the slick wood
of the rifle that stopped dozens of deer
before I was born. I pull the trigger again.

The buck takes two more steps
then drops, chest first, his back legs
holding firm, a brief argument
with fate. I approach. I want my father

to be here—to say *good shot*
or *well done*—so I won't feel
the heaving breaths of the dying deer.
My legs stutter. My father doesn't

come. The deer doesn't die,
and I don't know what to do
except hold my gun to the space
behind the buck's deep eye.

I tug the trigger, hoping
the soft chest will stop rising, compressing
the air as if to steal my breath
with each of his last. A fifth desperate shot

finds something important
in the throat. I'd tried the head
and chest. He kicks once
and settles in the dirt.

Above my buck's body,
I sway, nauseous, hoping my father
won't see the mess I've made,
the mess I've become.

The Long Madness

*Ian McKellen recently played the
title role in the Royal Shakespeare
Company's touring production of*
King Lear.

I saw Gandolf's staff
at the Guthrie

when Sir Ian
dropped his pants

in the 4-hour madness
of King Lear.

The Fool
picked them up,

but not before
the third-grader

next to me,
eyes, two wide balls,

like Gollum's, saw
the future,

the wrinkled future,
which hung

before us,
all glorious

and magical, foreshadowing
the ups and many downs.

THAT NIGHT IN MOBRIDGE

On the reservation when we spoke in tongues
as boys and I claimed to see an angel
outside our window, you said you saw it too,

but we didn't describe it
    (the sense of light in empty space
    the sense of bright form, indivisible)
for fear we were lying—today, for fear it was true.

You remind me we were boys, and I see
doubt swallowed you like candy sucked to nothing.
Now, I don't want to speak with you for fear

I'll be swallowed. Looking out the window
and seeing nothing, I ache for something
bright in all this darkness.

Xerxes' Queen

For if thou altogether holdest thy peace at this time . . .
thou and thy father's house shall be destroyed.
   —The Book of Esther

A grape in sunlight, warm and flushed, her cheek's
against her sovereign's thigh. He laughs and feasts
and orders men. She holds her tongue and speaks
a prayer inside, then lifts her head. A kiss of peace
to rouse him. Pressing lips to lips, she cries
and turns. Her fear ferments. He sobers, finds
she's aged a thousand years. Some death now lies
on her worn face. She speaks, her voice his wine.

For such a time as this, I speak as more
than lover, less than queen. My crown is dust,
and you, your majesty, will watch me bleed
my people's blood, a stain on Xerxes' floor—
or hang good Haman, he that thought it just
to steal from kings the touch and taste of queens.

Northern Peru

Before we ever went
to Chiclayo
and dressed as clowns
for orphans,
our leaders said
do not drink the water,
but the little boy
who took my first balloon
asked me three times
to share his orange popsicle,
pushing his sticky hand
above his head to mine.
I tasted it,
the sweet drip of orange
down both our chins.

Iowa Summer

Before meth's magic collapsed
your face, before you pimped
your girlfriend to pay for gas

and grass on your joyride
to Vegas, we mowed lawns
in Indianola to buy chips and

cherry cola from the corner sundry
and that Styrofoam airplane
to soar over the playground.

We hid behind the plastic
jungle, ate our Cool
Ranch Doritos, and with our toes

disappearing in sand, we stared
high above ourselves, wondering why
the wings blew off

and the whole thing turned
from the open sky and missiled
to the breaking ground.

The Things We Face

Through a tear in the little tent
outside the big one, I saw him
filch his face from a jar

and slap it on, like clay
on a wheel, centered on his cheeks
and molded up and down

to smooth the skin and tighten
jowls. He turned his hand 'round
his eyes to push away

the lines. And as if it were
the next step, before the lips
and eyes, the face, the white face,

an unburnished pot in the dust
and straw, toward me, it turned.

Winter Campout

Before the campers rose, we crawled
from our cocoon. David had let me sleep

in his bag—I'd forgot mine—
back to back and warm.

We didn't tell anyone or touch
the deep questions. In the icy night,

we peed out the side of our tent
into the tall and falling

snow. Two boy scouts, freezing,
spilled warm, twin yellow

arcs that melted holes but didn't
expose the earth, turning

in its white mask,
cold, and burning inside.

The Northern Mississippi

After St. Anthony Falls
under the Stone Arch Bridge,

the bounding river
is a thousand grasshoppers.

At 78, Maurita Discovers
the Waterslide

A German pear in a black one-piece
with a two-layer skirt to cover
some of her years, she doesn't know how
to go forward, sitting at the top
of the Black Tunnel. Loyle died

two months ago, and maybe he nudges her
from the beyond or the buildup
of water behind her finally lifts her
into the unknown. When they first met
61 years before the Parkinson's,

he lifeguarded at Crab Orchard Lake.
She took off her red cap when she walked
by so he'd see her blonde hair, now
as white as the sand on that beach.
He whooped like a crane

then looked away to pretend
he didn't feel an explosion. She smiled,
but today she whoops
and wails as the black water
surrounds her and turns her down

and around through tears and laughter.
She sees their beach that summer—Loyle
skims into the water to save her

from her parents, from all the boys
from Paducah to Carbondale, and from more

nights alone. They spooned
under Kentucky's tired sky for six decades.
She springs from the hole,
goes under and comes up baptized.
The crowd hears only the echo of her

screams. She listens only to her holy ghost
whooping back across the clear water. He still knows
what to say: *Maurita, you're Fifth Avenue.*

III.
Watershed

SIMULATIONS

I. POVERTY IDENTIFICATION SIMULATION

Dear Homeless People: You should know
that we, upper-middle-class college students,
will be wearing clothes
like yours. Some of us will even stink

like you by the third and final day of our project.
We'll probably sing Kum-Bay-Yah
and talk poverty. We'll shut off
our cell phones. One of us, probably a girl

from a suburb named something Falls,
will say, *I can't believe we'll be out here
all night*, and one of us, probably a boy with
gel in his hair, will snuggle up to the girl

and say, *It's so amazing how they live like this,
no homes or email, and they look for food
in dumpsters.* He'll look up at the spring night
we selected because it's not winter and whisper

like Nicolas Cage playing sad: *I'd do it,
look for food in the garbage.*
One of us, probably a lisping theology student
will say, *When my father lost his job*

*we would've been stuck on the streets
if my Grandpa hadn't owned a slew*

of rentals on the Southside. In a pallbearer's tone,
we'll talk about you people, how we know

what we're doing isn't *really* what you go through,
which will validate what we're doing. Before
we're resurrected from your world, one
of you, probably someone not as

dirty as we'd expect, will walk up to us as we
whisper, deciding who will address you.
How's it going? our spokesman will ask. You'll ask
for money, and we'll look at each other, something secret

validated within us. One of us, probably someone
with good teeth, will tell you, *We didn't bring money
'cause we're doing a poverty simulation.*
You'll look at us, at the holes

in our dark clothes, at our tap water bottles,
at our grouping together in threes and fours.
In your pocket you'll find some change and step
onto the next bus. One of us, probably most

of us, will question whether you are
really homeless. We won't know how to talk
of all that might be true. We'll finish
with pepperoni pizza back in the dorms.

II. POTHEAD PETE'S ENGLISH PRESENTATION

Shakespeare, the top American writer ever,
wrote his plays in an English accent
like Russell Crowe. *Merchant of Venice*

is a problem play because it's about hard crap
like racism and the civil rights movement,
but not Martin Luther King who was southern

and not in Boston like *the bard*,
which's Willie's nickname. People call me
Slash. Al Pacino's a character in the movie

adapted by Shakespeare just like the play,
except Shakespeare liked boys
to play girls, and no girls were allowed

in his theaters all over the globe. Even girl parts
like the chick who looks like Cate Blanchett,
who dresses like a boy—like Cate did

when she played Bob Dylan—that girl's named
after the car, Portia, to indicate she's wealthy—
even those girls were boys, but nobody was gay

back then—no offense. The Shylock wants
a pound of Jeremy Irons to pay for his sins
because Jews are going to hell

according to the Angel-Kind church, which is like
Catholics but their Pope gets divorced.
Queen Elizabeth, who still isn't dead,

banished the Jews. During the Holocaust
Hitler killed 6 million Jews. Israel was founded
in 1948. One scholar, Ilikeitlikethat74

on Cheatpapers.com suggested that Shakespeare
was racist and hired a ghost writer.
Build to a passionate close—oops,

I wasn't supposed to—that was my notes.
So we can learn much intelligence
from *Merchant* even if we don't know Jews

and we don't like Christians. In conclusion
a quote from Pacino, who starred
in *Scarface* and he was the devil

in that one with Keanu Reeves: "I am a Jew.
Hath not a Jew hands." I'll skip ahead
to stay under time, "If you prick us,

do we not bleed?" It's like, If you tickle us,
do we not laugh? In conclusion, you grasp
that Shakespeare is patriotic

and would have stood on the white cliffs
of Dover, Georgia with Dr. King.

III. POEM OF 4 EXPLANATIONS OF
POEMS AT POETRY READINGS

I.

by one of those ladies
with the red hats and purple shirts

I just wanna say
about this piece
you need to know
that I own 30 cats
and that the river
near my house is called Clementine
and so is my Siamese,
who appears in this poem
as one of my hats.

II.

by Doug, someone's roommate
until the body-shaving incident

This one is for a lady I called "mother"
in this poem, but my mother's here tonight,
Hi Mom, so we'll just say "Mother"
is a lady named Helga
but for the sake of the poem's integrity
we'll still say "Mother." Entitled
"I hate your face."

III.
by the wide-eyed guy
nobody has ever seen before

Before I got out of prison
me and the guys in my cell
wrote a poem about dancing
that resonates with me
so if we could all stand together
and hold hands and think
of death row—I'll read
"The last dance of innocent Rico."

IV.
by a lit. major named Shirley
with the dark black hair

This poem totally speaks
for itself so I don't need to tell you anything
except in book II of Paradise Lost
when Satan must move through
Hell's mouth he meets
his wife slash daughter Sin
and son slash Sin's lover, Death.
Oh, and the color red symbolizes blood.

Safety

I. Evander Holyfield's Left Ear Remembers June 28, 1997

I could see the trouble
in Tyson's ears
at center ring:
two tiny lobes
playing dumb.
Gloves touched,

then Holy's jab
danced on Tyson's
face through round
one and two,
one-two, one-two.

Right got the first bite,
a toddler's nip,
a lover's clench,
a light scratch
for two points.
His upper cut

caught me, just
an ear, like thunder
and pushed past
to the wide, wide
air above. His iron
bite dropped me

to the canvas
and I couldn't
hear myself
scream through
the veil
of blood and spit.
Submerged in fight,

Tyson hadn't caught
his corner's *Use the jab*,
the crowd's *Iron Mike*
and *Holyfield*,
or Mills Lane's
Keep it clean.

They wrapped me
in a latex glove,
and carried me,
knocked out and
bloody, back
to my head.

I could see
the trouble
in his ears,
two tiny lobes
on a mad bull
in a crowd, in a world
waving red.

II. COLEMAN GENERATOR PLANT
—DARRELL, LINE SUPERVISOR

Some girl in Florida better be able to play Nintendo
when the power goes out. Stand here—
take the copper wires like so. Don't touch that button

with your elbow. Fix your fingers
on the base, and kick the switch on the spreader,
not with your left foot or you'll trip

the sensor. Turn the wires 45 degrees
toward the gap on the inserter, press firm
like you're holding down a rabid Rottweiler,

not too close or it'll bite, and you'll get
a thumb nub like this one—ain't as bad
as Mooch's. He lopped off one

and a half on his good hand, hopped around
like a retarded bunny. Some of his blood's
still under the lid. Son, generators don't build

themselves. Pick up the core from the line—
they're usually 43 pounds, but they'll get up
to 85 on the biggest beasts—move it

to the inserter, and don't let the papers stick out—
nobody gets the bonus if we don't
get them papers right. Drink plenty

of water or you'll pass out, crack your head
on the concrete. There ain't no air conditioner,
so you'll sweat your weight in half a day.

Keep up the wire and the papers, but don't sweat
the blocks running out. Carl's on the line—
you'll have blocks all day. Pull it off

the inserter—start her down the line. If you don't
know nothing, ask Pedro—he's from Peru
or somewhere down there. He don't do English,

but he'll tell you when you screw up. I'll see you
in two breaks and 12 hours. If you break
those safety glasses you have to pay for new ones.

III. My Uncle Learns Me How to Keep
a Mechanic from Screwing Me Over

Because you can say *carburetor*
don't mean you can say it
with a mechanic's accent. They'll smell

your fugazi butt if you spin their words
without accenting the right syllables
like how a doctor gets all Johns Hopkins—

saying *GI track* fast like you don't know
he doesn't mean joining the Marines.
My second cousin Perth from Norway

ended up, one month stateside,
with a colon tube or something
like that from a big IQ MD, and a new head

gasket from Vinny's Auto for his half-dead
VW Rabbit when he tried to pass
like he'd read books

about meds and cars. For two weeks, he slept
on his stomach in an Ikea futon
and couldn't order pizza

because a head gasket's like 500 bucks
with labor. Don't smile at a man
with grease on his hands. Keep your face

stern like you know something about something
and you know he knows something
about something you don't know. Straight

respect, like the Bible with Jews.
I always tell 'em *it's my kid's car*
and I'm hoping to get it worked on

before he gets back from Iraq. Can you imagine
Ricky in Iraq? He'd get sand in his eyes
and pee himself. You're probably too young

to say something about a kid
in the war. So maybe say *my mechanic's sick*
with the cancer so he can't look at it till next week

when he's between chemo. Oh, always end
by asking casually, like a doc says
turn your head and cough, like it don't

matter to nobody, *are you guys*
still servicing the cop cars? It's like the Soviets
used to do to make people stand in line

for bread or to make their red doctors
stick a horse heart in an East German
swimmer so she'll turn turbo in the pool.

SHADOWS THAT MIGHT CATCH FIRE

I. BILL BITNER AT THE HENRY DOORLY ZOO

The rhino likes to hide off to the left, behind
the brown sign and the Africa brush,
but I know where to wait

so I alone can see the beast push
its whale's eye and hairy victrola ears
toward the water. I won't drink my water

till he drinks. It's a battle of will—Rhino
and Bill Bitner. One time I drank
a gallon of milk and threw up

on some college guys. They said I was too stupid
to drink the whole thing. At the first digging
of hooves in dirt, I hold my ears out

with my hands, and my tired eyes
get wide. My rash tingles, pushes me
toward the fence, toward the tip of grey horn

that sticks out into the space
between leaves. I giggle to the fence,
That head's like a Volkswagen bug, so big,

so big. People stay away
from the angle I've found. They don't know
what I know. I call mother from the pay phone

by the orangutans. Sweating and stammering,
I say, *Momma, I petted a rhino*, and she doesn't
believe me when I describe the prickly skin

and the lonely eyes. I hang up and walk
wild through the gift shop toward the exit,
stopping only to put back

a stuffed dog knocked on the ground.

II. Bill Bitner Goes to Walmart

My smile's always a half-grin turned up like a clown's.
Eyes to the front, I'm an undercover fed who has to score

some crack. The happy-yellow-sticker lady looks past me
toward a lost balloon stuck to the metal ceiling,

about to pop. I keep walking, right hand close to my pocket
and the left swinging free as a wind chime. Nobody knows

what Bill Bitner knows. I grab three kinds of soap
because only one says white. It might be too white,

and I can't see the color of the Irish Spring. The lady
with the blue vest, lines on her face and cigarette teeth

looks at me like she knows something when I ask
if the soap is off-white or white. I don't say thanks.

I'm thinking of how I'll cut it into pieces
and put it in a plastic bag on my seat, hoping to get

pulled over doing 60 in a 45 with soap that looks like crack.
I'll just grin when a cop thinks anything at all.

I'll keep my mouth shut about the feds and the job
and the nights when Bill Bitner isn't safe.

III. Bill Bitner Meets Subway's Jared

I shouldn't have punched him,
but those jeans weren't scuffed
around the heel or thin
in the thigh where fat should rub them.
Nobody took the time
to check that one fat
Jared picture probably Photoshopped
by some commercial people.
I had a poster of Jared
on my bathroom wall above
where I pee, and in 2001,
when my prostate infection
flared, I stared at the pants
for long moments and swore
to expose the truth between
sharp pains and short bursts.
It was an easy recall when,
across the street in Indianapolis,
the plump pants were being
folded outside an auditorium,
and I jaywalked, screaming
"Jared" like a battle cry.
My fist cracked the jaw
of some comedian who 'personates
Bill Clinton better than Jared.
In a ceremony the next day

I burned the poster
and a meatball sub and wore
my own size 44 pants
around my head like a warrior.

IV. BILL BITNER SMELLS

Mother rebounded home on Saturdays
from her truck route. Her rig parked
on the sunken lawn. She was the only one
who opened my window in the morning before
I woke. The wind pulled in them thick lilacs
and mixed with Mother's cigarettes. She'd sit
on my bed, working out her logbook, flicking ashes
onto the painted floor, glancing up
at me pretending to sleep.

I rigged a CB to my bucket of bolts
bicycle a few years back, but the batteries
got expensive, and I left it in the rain
outside my apartment. Last March I took it off
for good. I return the trucker's call
in my head. *Wild Bill, what's your twenty?*
Plugged in to a timer, set to 5 a.m.,
my Glade Plug-In smokes a lilac scent.
Wild Bill, Wild Bill?
Are you playing dead? Over.

V. Bill Bitner's Bundle of Something Identical

Once a month or so, I go to the Econo Lodge
and drop off a bundle, usually a wrapped-up phone book
or something else heavy, before the sun gets up.

To the nametag on the lady, I say, *My brother*
will come around to pick this up. It's something important.
He looks a lot like me, but his voice is higher.

Mother, more than once, told me I got
my brother's name. Bill Bitner the First, my older
twin, caught something blue and died 10 minutes old.

When the sun sticks through the slits on the west window
and bounces off the TV screen, I get up
from my plaid chair and pull my fishing hat down on my eyes.

I fix a limp or stutter step onto my legs when I see
the same lady at the counter. *I'm here to pick something up*
from my brother. My voice usually cracks on *brother.*

Your brother, Mother said, *probably would've been a foot taller,*
able to digest peanuts, and eczema free. I wonder if Bill
would have been afraid of shadows that might catch fire.

The lady gives me the package like she's found a teddy bear
and I'm its child. It's a phone book. I take it, hold it close to my heart
murmur, and forget to ask what I really want to know—

When I dropped this off, what was my name?

VI. Bill Bitner Tells Bear Stories

Out of the woods, I come to tell bear stories
to Cub Scouts when they camp on Terry Ridge
and their leader gets into the van

to talk on his tiny phone. *Look, it's Bill Bitner,*
they laugh. I say, I tell bear stories. They look up
at me—*Bill Bitner, tell us a bear story*—

like I'm Regis. I start when they beg: *Bill Bitner,
we'll give you a s'more and let you stoke the fire.*
A camper sat on the edge of a log, carving a stick

into a hot dog spear—I tell this one at the campfire
when they just ate hot dogs. He stopped. Something
made his skin bump up like the gooses.

There's a whistling behind him. He turned
real slow-like, knife in one hand, stick in the other.
A bear was eating his friend. Red and grey guts

were sprung open, and the only sound was the whistle
of his buddy's lungs as the bear shook him
like a wet towel. Sssssst. Sssssst—I do it like that,

Ssssst, maybe six times—He tried to stab the bear,
but the bear killed 'em both. Bears don't know
what they're doing sometimes.

They found them bodies split in two on Terry Ridge.
They never done did found that bear.

VII. Bill Bitner Delivers Pizza

You don't have clothes on your naked parts,
I said to the tall lady who ordered
a large with Canada ham
and pineapples. She asked, *Why*

do they call it Hawaiian?, her voice
like a squished mouse. Maybe in Hawaii
they only eat pizza like yours, I said,
and they get pigs real cheap

from Canada. Pineapples are beautiful fruit
like prickly Mr. Potato Heads except
with juice—real juicy—and that poky top thing
that looks like a plant hat. Why don't you

have no clothes? She still was naked and didn't
answer. One hand up on the door,
the other on her hip, she made
a little teapot. She never did take the pizza

or give me a tip. I said to the boss,
the guy with the net on his beard, there's a naked
lady, and I'm not gonna take any more
pizzas—Bill Bitner quits. I might stop back

on Thursday, but I won't expect nothing
free. Bill Bitner will have the special
with sticks. She looked like
a big smooth rock in the river.

VIII. Bill Bitner Explains His Qualifications for the C.I.A. to the Hot Jobs Temp Agency

I couldn't stop scratching under my thigh
where the rash is always the worst.
   I have a tazer in my pocket
   and I shocked myself like the cops do.
I remembered how tazers felt
like fifty fuzzy bee stings as I stared
at the mustache on the man afraid
to smile in the interview seat.
   I can keep a secret, like if you told me
   you were drinking on the job
   or you like to wear women's panties,
   I wouldn't say nothing to somebody.
   I once stole a brownie from a bake sale
   for a lady with cancer. It was in her eye.
The man leaned toward me
and had nothing to say, like a drop of water
that don't plop. I stopped scratching
and leaned toward him. Bill Bitner took charge:
   I read "The Nasty Little Englishmen," the story
   of Churchill and about his blood, sweat, tears,
   so I understand about the commitment
   except not about England. I don't like England.
   I read about black ops on the Internet,
   no connections—I wouldn't even exist.
   Is this interview one of those tests,
   like would I kill my mother?

IX. Bill Bitner Rides Again

I got five bucks and I want you
to taxi me to the statue lady
with the torch, I growl to the black man
sitting on beads. He says, *Five ain't enough*

*for two blocks, and she got her own
island.* I say, I got here yesterday
to meet Pricilla47, my computer
match, who'd said I could sleep on her

couch in the city. Then we met
and she marched out of JoJo's Pizza,
tossing the rose Mother recommended
in the can. I feel like New York

and the other coast—I see 'em
like death dreams—they keep pushing
toward the middle, soaking
the safe ground, swearing Bill Bitner

should bask in the oceans' misty wisdom.
Misty wisdom—that's from Hawkeye
on *M.A.S.H.*, I think. I don't think
the ocean knows much. The cab says, *Get out*

if you ain't got more money. Pricilla didn't
say sorry that she didn't love anymore.
She turned back, her face a bright screen
in the dark—*I don't do no Midwestern Jester.*

Her chubby hips went out the door
like a heifer ramblin' to pasture. I forgot
to say something back, just sat there, a wolf
howling, growling at the fire he's afraid to touch.

X. Bill Bitner Attends His Grandfather's Funeral

I keep getting back in the line to see the body,
waiting for the people who aren't really looking

to turn away long enough so I can put my finger
on the nose, which most of all looks like a shiny

sunken ship. The makeup rubs off, and the wreck
loses the shiny in the dry spot only I can see

under those dim chapel lights. I don't sit
with the family. They didn't let me vote

on the details: where to put the flowers, who
should sing the songs, and how to keep Grandpa's face

looking alive in a casket which I would very much like
to close. When the minister starts rambling, I notice

my finger and rub Pa's makeup on my cheek.
The salty water washes it clean. We're mingling

right here, and nobody can stop it.

XI. BILL BITNER
DAYDREAMS

I want to sell
hot dogs for
a day from a
corner in the
city where
everyone says
I'll have the
works, to turn
the meat
tubes in hot
water with
long tongs,
and to stink
like mustard
and relish the
scream: *Hot*
dogs, get your
hot dogs, like
everyone
needs me
to stay alive.

XII. BILL BITNER'S BASKETBALL

The fence between the trailer court and the hoop
had holes near them fat bushes. I'd crawl—sometimes
I got thorn cut, but that's war for you—

and sink through the chain lengths
like a ball through the net. In fifth grade,
I stole a shiny white and red football

from Bobby Calkevekie's shed
and carried it through the prickly space
to the cracked slab where the big boys

were lions with balls. I growled, *Anyone
can dribble a round ball.* They laughed
watching me bounce and fall around the field

shooting the ball in the net, sometimes.
Probably nobody has ever played the game
I played. The unflated ball sits on my TV,

and when anyone asks, *Bill Bitner, what's with
the dead ball?* I grin, proud as a bomb:
It's from my basketball days! Then, as one

of the game's old soldiers, I look toward the skies,
try to remember battles, grab my knee,
wince, and close my eyes till I see backwards.

Biographical Note

Gary Dop—poet, performer, and playwright—lives in the foothills of Virginia's Blue Ridge Mountains, where he is an English professor at Randolph College. Dop received his MFA from the University of Nebraska, and his writing, which has been published throughout the country in magazines such as *Prairie Schooner, Poetry Northwest, Agni*, and *New Letters*, has been recognized with a Pushcart Prize Special Mention and the 2013 Great Plains Emerging Writer Prize.